What you wi

CW00468918

1.   Initial Information
2.   Updated, clear picture{s}
3.   Any information for Contacts
4. Car{s} makes. models, vin, tag and insurance information
5.   Pictures of tatoos or scars, or detailed information about any identifying marks
6.   Social Media usernames and passwords
7.   Bank information/Credit Card information
8.   Updated Section for daily "I am going here"
9. Any information on people who might be upset with you or want to cause you harm
10. Any extra information that might be helpful

Initial Information

All of your information:
Name {full legal name and any that have been used in the past. Address {home and work}, Phone numbers {cell, house, work}

Initial Information

All of your information:
Name {full legal name and any that have been used in the past. Address {home and work}, Phone numbers {cell, house, work}

Pictures of me

Add as many updated pictures as you can.
Make them large and clear.
Have a few just of your face with different profiles.

Pictures of me

Add as many updated pictures as you
can.
Make them large and clear.
Have a few just of your face with
different profiles.

Pictures of me

Add as many updated pictures as you
can.
Make them large and clear.
Have a few just of your face with
different profiles.

Pictures of me

Add as many updated pictures as you can.
Make them large and clear.
Have a few just of your face with different profiles.

Pictures of me

Add as many updated pictures as you
can.
Make them large and clear.
Have a few just of your face with
different profiles.

Contacts

3

Emergency Contact information,
friends that you hang out with often, family and co-workers. Include names,
phone numbers and addresses. Give as much info as possible.

3 Contacts

Emergency Contact information,
friends that you hang out with often, family and co-workers. Include names,
phone numbers and addresses. Give as much info as possible.

Contacts

3

Emergency Contact information,
friends that you hang out with often, family and co-workers. Include names,
phone numbers and addresses. Give as much info as possible.

Contacts

Emergency Contact information,
friends that you hang out with often, family and co-workers. Include names,
phone numbers and addresses. Give as much info as possible.

3 Contacts

Emergency Contact information,
friends that you hang out with often, family and co-workers. Include names,
phone numbers and addresses. Give as much info as possible.

Vehicle Information

Any info on vehicles you own. Cars, trucks, suv's,
mobile or motor homes, motorcycles ect..
Add Vin and tag numbers, makes and models and
insurance information. Include pictures if possible.

Vehicle Information

Any info on vehicles you own. Cars, trucks, suv's,
mobile or motor homes, motorcycles ect..
Add Vin and tag numbers, makes and models and
insurance information. Include pictures if possible.

Vehicle Information

Any info on vehicles you own. Cars, trucks, suv's,
mobile or motor homes, motorcycles ect..
Add Vin and tag numbers, makes and models and
insurance information. Include pictures if possible.

Vehicle Information

Any info on vehicles you own. Cars, trucks, suv's,
mobile or motor homes, motorcycles ect..
Add Vin and tag numbers, makes and models and
insurance information. Include pictures if possible.

Vehicle Information

Any info on vehicles you own. Cars, trucks, suv's, mobile or motor homes, motorcycles ect..
Add Vin and tag numbers, makes and models and insurance information. Include pictures if possible.

Vehicle Information

Any info on vehicles you own. Cars, trucks, suv's, mobile or motor homes, motorcycles ect..
Add Vin and tag numbers, makes and models and insurance information. Include pictures if possible.

Body Markers

5

Add any information on tattoos, scars, missing teeth or limbs. Any surgeries etc. Add pictures of tattoos and scars if possible. Give descriptive information.

⑤ Body Markers

Add any information on tattoos, scars, missing teeth or limbs. Any surgeries etc. Add pictures of tattoos and scars if possible. Give descriptive information.

Body Markers

5

Add any information on tattoos, scars, missing teeth or limbs. Any surgeries etc. Add pictures of tattoos and scars if possible. Give descriptive information.

Body Markers

5 Add any information on tattoos, scars, missing teeth or limbs. Any surgeries etc. Add pictures of tattoos and scars if possible. Give descriptive information.

5 Body Markers

Add any information on tattoos, scars, missing teeth or limbs. Any surgeries etc. Add pictures of tattoos and scars if possible. Give descriptive information.

⑤ Body Markers

Add any information on tattoos, scars, missing teeth or limbs. Any surgeries etc. Add pictures of tattoos and scars if possible. Give descriptive information.

Usernames and Passwords

Give usernames and passwords for laptops, tablets, phones, etc. Give usernames and passwords for social media, email accounts etc.

Usernames and Passwords

Give usernames and passwords for laptops, tablets, phones, etc. Give usernames and passwords for social media, email accounts etc.

Usernames and Passwords

Give usernames and passwords for laptops, tablets, phones, etc. Give usernames and passwords for social media, email accounts etc.

Usernames and Passwords

Give usernames and passwords for laptops, tablets, phones, etc. Give usernames and passwords for social media, email accounts etc.

Usernames and Passwords

Give usernames and passwords for laptops, tablets, phones, etc. Give usernames and passwords for social media, email accounts etc.

Bank and Credit Information

Add bank and credit card info
for police to keep a check on
accounts.

Bank and Credit Information
Add bank and credit card info
for police to keep a check on
accounts.

Bank and Credit Information
Add bank and credit card info
for police to keep a check on
accounts.

Bank and Credit Information
Add bank and credit card info
for police to keep a check on
accounts.

Bank and Credit Information

Add bank and credit card info
for police to keep a check on
accounts.

Daily Update

Add info if you are going anywhere outside of your routine. Who you are going with and the contact info for them, with as many details as possible

Daily Update

Add info if you are going anywhere outside of your routine. Who you are going with and the contact info for them, with as many details as possible

Daily Update

Add info if you are going anywhere outside of your routine. Who you are going with and the contact info for them, with as many details as possible

Daily Update

Add info if you are going anywhere outside of your routine. Who you are going with and the contact info for them, with as many details as possible

Daily Update

Add info if you are going anywhere outside of your routine. Who you are going with and the contact info for them, with as many details as possible

Daily Update

Add info if you are going anywhere outside of your routine. Who you are going with and the contact info for them, with as many details as possible

Daily Update

Add info if you are going anywhere outside of your routine. Who you are going with and the contact info for them, with as many details as possible

Daily Update

Add info if you are going anywhere outside of your routine. Who you are going with and the contact info for them, with as many details as possible

Daily Update

Add info if you are going anywhere outside of your routine. Who you are going with and the contact info for them, with as many details as possible

Daily Update

Add info if you are going anywhere outside of your routine. Who you are going with and the contact info for them, with as many details as possible

Daily Update

Add info if you are going anywhere outside of your routine. Who you are going with and the contact info for them, with as many details as possible

Daily Update

Add info if you are going anywhere outside of your routine. Who you are going with and the contact info for them, with as many details as possible

Is someone upset with me?

Info on anyone who might be upset with you, add if you have had any arguments recently, or anything wierd you may have seen from someone. Be detailed.

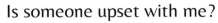

Is someone upset with me?

Info on anyone who might be upset with you, add if you have had any arguments recently, or anything wierd you may have seen from someone. Be detailed.

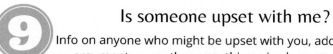

Is someone upset with me?

Info on anyone who might be upset with you, add if you have had any arguments recently, or anything wierd you may have seen from someone. Be detailed.

Is someone upset with me?

Info on anyone who might be upset with you, add if you have had any arguments recently, or anything wierd you may have seen from someone. Be detailed.

Is someone upset with me?

Info on anyone who might be upset with you, add if you have had any arguments recently, or anything wierd you may have seen from someone. Be detailed.

Is someone upset with me?

Info on anyone who might be upset with you, add if you have had any arguments recently, or anything wierd you may have seen from someone. Be detailed.

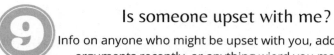

Is someone upset with me?

Info on anyone who might be upset with you, add if you have had any arguments recently, or anything wierd you may have seen from someone. Be detailed.

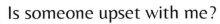

Is someone upset with me?

Info on anyone who might be upset with you, add if you have had any
arguments recently, or anything wierd you may have seen from
someone. Be detailed.

Extra

Any extra info or pictures that may be helpful in a Just in Case kind of way!

Extra

Any extra info or pictures that may be helpful in a Just in Case kind of way!

Extra

Any extra info or pictures that may be helpful in a Just in Case kind of way!

Extra

Any extra info or pictures that may be helpful in a Just in Case kind of way!

Extra

Any extra info or pictures that may be helpful in a Just in Case kind of way!

Extra

Any extra info or pictures that may be helpful in a Just in Case kind of way!

Extra

Any extra info or pictures that may be helpful in a Just in Case kind of way!

Extra

Any extra info or pictures that may be helpful in a Just in Case kind of way!

Extra

Any extra info or pictures that may be helpful in a Just in Case kind of way!

Extra

Any extra info or pictures that may be helpful in a Just in Case kind of way!

Extra

Any extra info or pictures that may be helpful in a Just in Case kind of way!

Extra

Any extra info or pictures that may be helpful in a Just in Case kind of way!

Extra

Any extra info or pictures that may be helpful in a Just in Case kind of way!

Extra

Any extra info or pictures that may
be helpful in a Just in Case kind of
way!

STAY SAFE